The Respiratory System

by Helen Frost

Consulting Editor: Gail Saunders-Smith, Ph.D.

Consultant: Lawrence M. Ross, M.D., Ph.D.
Member, American Association of Clinical Anatomists

Pebble Books

an imprint of Capstone Press
Mankato, Minnesota

Pebble Books are published by Capstone Press
151 Good Counsel Drive, P.O. Box 669, Mankato, Minnesota 56002
http://www.capstone-press.com

Library of Congress Cataloging-in-Publication Data
Frost, Helen, 1949–
    The respiratory system/by Helen Frost.
    p. cm.—(Human body systems)
    Includes bibliographical references and index.
    Summary: Simple text, photographs, and diagrams introduce the respiratory
system, its purpose, parts, and functions.
    ISBN 0-7368-0652-0
    1. Respiratory organs—Juvenile literature. [1. Respiratory system.] I. Title.
II. Human body systems (Mankato, Minn.)
QM251 .F76 2001
612.2—dc21

00-024557

Note to Parents and Teachers

The Human Body Systems series supports national science
standards for units on understanding the basic functions of the
human body. This book describes the respiratory system and
illustrates its purpose, parts, and functions. The photographs and
diagrams support early readers in understanding the text. This
book also introduces early readers to subject-specific vocabulary
words, which are defined in the Words to Know section. Early
readers may need assistance to read some words and to use the
Table of Contents, Words to Know, Read More, Internet Sites, and
Index/Word List sections of the book.

Table of Contents

The respiratory system helps people breathe. It brings fresh air into the body. The respiratory system takes away air that has been used.

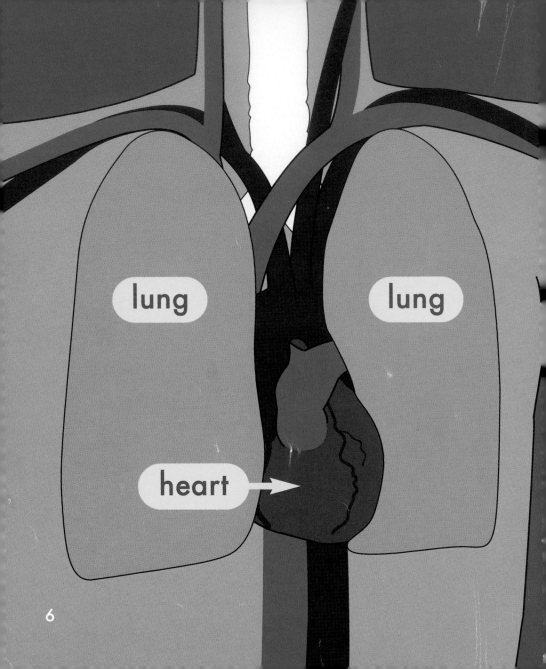

lung

lung

heart

People have two lungs.
One lung is on each side
of the heart.

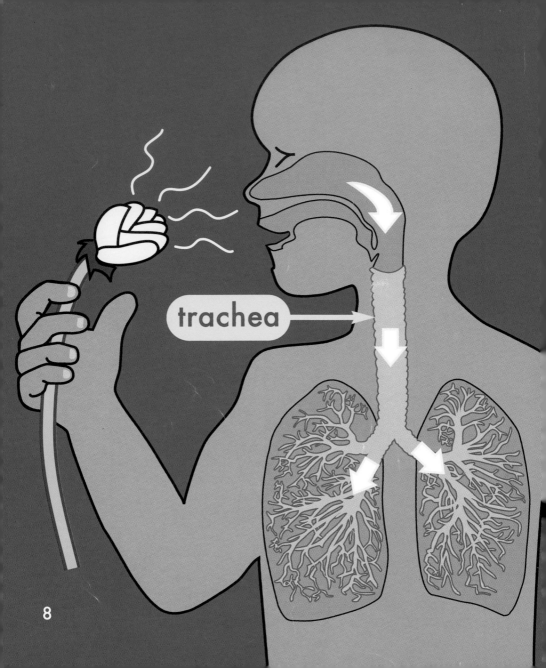

trachea

People breathe in air through the mouth and nose. The air goes into the trachea. This tube connects the mouth and nose to the lungs.

The trachea splits into two large airways. Each airway goes to one lung. The airways split into smaller and smaller airways inside the lungs.

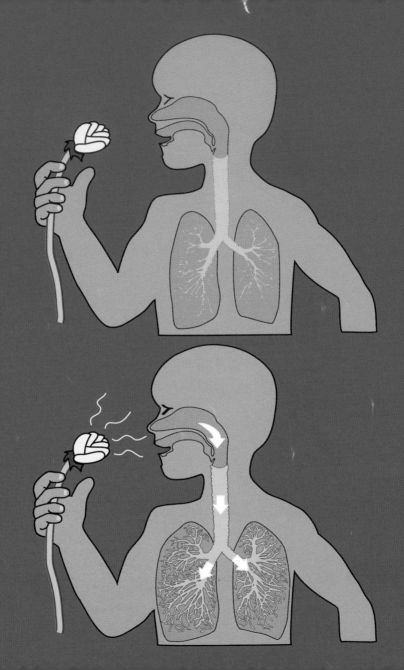

Air goes through the airways into the lungs. The air makes the lungs bigger.

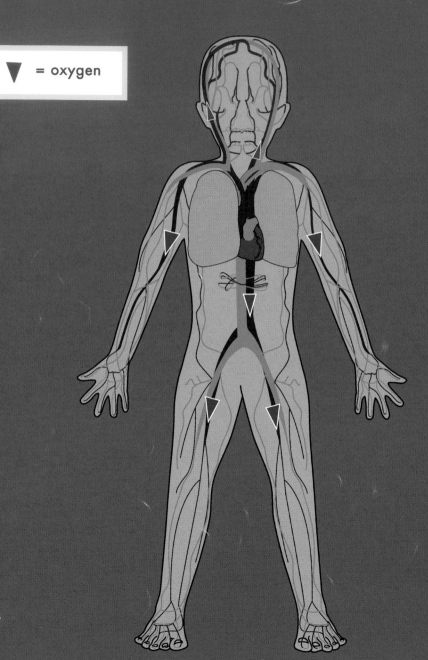

Air has a gas called oxygen. All parts of the body need oxygen. Blood picks up oxygen from the lungs. The blood takes the oxygen to the body through blood vessels.

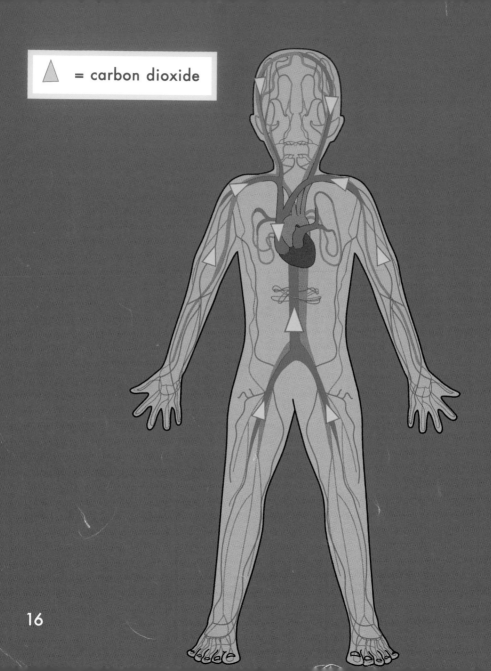

= carbon dioxide

16

Blood picks up a gas called carbon dioxide from the body. Blood returns to the lungs with the carbon dioxide. The body does not need carbon dioxide. Blood leaves carbon dioxide in the lungs.

People breathe out through the mouth and nose. The carbon dioxide goes out of the body. The lungs get smaller as the air leaves the body.

Air leaving the body goes through the larynx. People use the larynx to make sounds. The larynx helps people speak and sing.

Words to Know

breathe—to take air in and out of the lungs

carbon dioxide—a gas that people breathe out; plants take in carbon dioxide because they need it to live.

larynx—the upper part of the trachea; the larynx holds the vocal cords; it also is called the voice box.

lung—a body part inside the chest; air goes into the lungs when people breathe in; lungs have little pockets of tissue to hold air; lungs have many blood vessels.

oxygen—a gas found in the air; oxygen has no color or smell; people and animals need oxygen to live.

trachea—a tube that connects the mouth and nose to the lungs; air goes in and out of the body through the trachea; the trachea also is called the windpipe.

Read More

Cromwell, Sharon. *Why Can't I Breathe Underwater?: And Other Questions about the Respiratory System.* Body Wise. Des Plaines, Ill.: Rigby, 1998.

Furgang, Kathy. *My Lungs.* My Body. New York: PowerKids Press, 2000.

Parker, Steve. *Lungs.* Look at Your Body. Brookfield, Conn.: Copper Beech Books, 1996.

Stille, Darlene R. *The Respiratory System.* A True Book. New York: Children's Press, 1997.

Internet Sites

Looking at Your Lungs
http://kidshealth.org/kid/body/lungs_noSW.html

Respiratory System: The Air Bags
http://www.imcpl.lib.in.us/nov_resp.htm

Welcome to the Respiratory System
http://tqjunior.advanced.org/5777/resp1.htm

Your Gross and Cool Body—Respiratory System
http://www.yucky.com/body/index.ssf?/
systems/respiratory

Index/Word List

air, 5, 9, 13, 15, 19, 21
airway, 11, 13
blood, 15, 17
blood vessels, 15
body, 5, 15, 17, 19, 21
breathe, 5, 9, 19
carbon dioxide, 17, 19
heart, 7

larynx, 21
lung, 7, 9, 11, 13, 15, 17, 19
mouth, 9, 19
nose, 9, 19
oxygen, 15
people, 7, 19, 21
respiratory system, 5
sounds, 21
trachea, 9, 11

Word Count: 212
Early-Intervention Level: 17

Editorial Credits
Martha E. H. Rustad, editor; Kia Bielke, designer; Marilyn Moseley LaMantia, Graphicstock, illustrator; Katy Kudela, photo researcher

Photo Credits
Index Stock Imagery, 1, 18
Marilyn Moseley LaMantia, 10
Shaffer Photography/James L. Shaffer, cover
Unicorn Stock Photos/Ed Harp, 4; Jeff Greenberg, 20

The author thanks the children's section staff at the Allen County Public Library in Fort Wayne, Indiana, for research assistance. The author also thanks Linda Hathaway, CFCS, Health Educator, McMillen Center for Health Education, Fort Wayne, Indiana.

BAG